SAVING OUR
WETLANDS
AND THEIR
WILDLIFE

By Karen Liptak

FRANKLIN WATTS

New York | London | Toronto | Sydney
A First Book | 1991

Cover photograph courtesy of Jeff Foott Productions

Photographs courtesy of: Comstock Inc.: pp. 8, 10, 12 bottom, 27, 31 (all Townsend P. Dickinson), 12 top, 49 (both Dr. Georg Gerster), 14 top (Denver Bryan), 25 bottom (Phyllis Greenberg); DRK Photo: pp. 14 bottom, 17 bottom (both Wayne Lankinen), 21 top (John Eastcott/Yva Momatiuk), 44 (S. Nielsen), 47, 50 (both Marty Cordano); Frederick D. Atwood: pp. 17 top, 21 bottom; Jeff Foott Productions: pp. 18, 34, 39, 42; Louisiana Geological Survey/Karen Westphal: p. 23; Wade C. Sherbrooke: p. 25 top; U.S. Fish and Wildlife Service: pp. 29 top (Chincoteague National Wildlife Refuge/Michael Colopy), 29 bottom (Benvenuti).

Library of Congress Cataloging-in-Publication Data

Liptak, Karen.
  Saving our wetlands and their wildlife / Karen Liptak.
    p.   cm. — (A First book)
  Includes bibliographical references and index.
  Summary: Describes different types of wetlands and their wildlife, including endangered plants and animals, explaining the environmental threats to the wetlands themselves.
    ISBN 0-531-20092-2
    1. Wetlands—United States—Juvenile literature.   2. Wetland conservation—United States—Juvenile literature.   3. Wetland ecology—United States—Juvenile literature.   [1. Wetlands.   2. Wetland ecology.   3. Ecology.   4. Conservation of natural resources.]   I. Title.   II. Series.
QH104.L57   1991
333.91′8—dc20   91-4682
                                                                                                                          CIP
First Paperback Edition 1992   AC
0-531-15648-6

MY SPECIAL THANKS to these dedicated people who graciously shared their love and knowledge about our wetlands: Dr. Roy Johnson, University of Arizona; Dr. Henry Murkins, Dick Wentz, Ken Boettcher, and Sunny Mowbray, Ducks Unlimited; Keren Larson and Dr. Michael Carrie, Sierra Club; Paul Parks, Florida Wildlife Federation; Dan Campbell, The Nature Conservancy; Tanna Thornburgh, Arizona Parks Department; Linda Winter, The Izaak Walton League of America; and anyone I am inadvertently forgetting.

CONTENTS

SAVING OUR WETLANDS AND THEIR WILDLIFE

A typical saltwater marsh

OUR WONDERFUL WETLANDS

Our nation's wetlands are among its most important natural areas. Wetlands are crucial to a great diversity of wildlife, including many rare and endangered plants and animals. Wetlands are also vital to people—these wet and spongy places perform several natural functions that benefit us all.

Yet many wetlands are vanishing today. For a long time, people thought of them as smelly, disease-infested wastelands that should be filled in. We have only recently come to realize our wetlands' true worth and why they must be saved.

TYPES OF WETLANDS

Wetlands are found all over our country and come in many forms. There are both freshwater and saltwater wetlands. Freshwater wetlands are found inland, while

9

saltwater wetlands are located along seacoasts. Coastal wetlands are closely linked with *estuaries*, places where salt water from the sea mixes with fresh water from rivers. Estuaries serve as important nurseries for many kinds of fish.

The most familiar wetlands are swamps and marshes. *Swamps* are soggy places dominated by trees. *Marshes* are treeless areas, with low-lying plants that can live in soils saturated with water. Swamps and marshes can be saltwater or freshwater. Other fresh-water wetlands include bogs, bottomlands, prairie potholes, and riparian areas. *Bogs*, places with wet, spongy ground, usually support a kind of moss known as *sphagnum*. This rootless plant can soak up over a hundred times its own weight in water!

Bottomlands, also called bottomland hardwood forests, are commonly found along streams and rivers on flood plains. *Prairie potholes* are shallow, marshlike ponds located primarily in the Midwest. *Riparian* (from the Latin word *ripa*, meaning "bank") wetlands are the banks along any inland body of water, and are even found in the desert Southwest. Each kind of wetland has a unique *ecosystem*, or balance of plants and animals, that depends upon it for survival.

Wetlands are important to the balance of nature. This is a freshwater marsh in Maine.

Above: A coastal estuary in Louisiana where salt water from the Gulf of Mexico mixes with fresh water from rivers.

Left: Sphagnum moss has no roots and acts like a sponge, soaking up water from the bogs where it grows.

We need our wetlands for many reasons. Wetlands are among the most productive natural ecosystems on earth. They produce great quantities of plants, some of which could not live anywhere else. These plants include cattails, saw grasses, and rushes, as well as mangrove and cypress trees and a variety of wild flowers. Many wetland plants provide food, shelter, and nesting areas for the animals that also call the wetlands their home.

Wetlands are the major breeding grounds and migrating stopovers for waterfowl (ducks, geese, and swans) and other birds, including a magnificent array of wading birds and shorebirds. Herons, egrets, and wood storks (or ibis) need the wetlands. So, too, do rails, coots, gallinules, and many songbirds.

Some amphibians, such as frogs and salamanders, and many reptiles, including snakes and tortoises, rely upon the wetlands. Here, too, can be found mammals such as marsh rabbits, muskrats, and mice. The wetlands are also shared by a multitude of insects, as well as clams, snails, and crabs.

But wetlands aren't just unique wildlife habitats. They are also Mother Earth's natural reservoirs. When rain and snow sink into the ground, they are stored in

Above: Ducks and other water-fowl use wetlands as resting places during their migrations and as breeding grounds.

Left: Wetlands are natural habitats for mammals such as this muskrat.

natural underground "tubs" in the wetlands. This prevents the water from immediately heading through the river system and out into the sea. Later, this water reserve can be pumped up by humans as it is needed.

Wetlands also help to control flooding. When floodwaters come, the heavy, spongy vegetation of many wetlands absorbs the water and helps to slow its flow.

Wetlands are useful as natural sewage systems, too. Certain wetlands vegetation can filter wastes out of the streams that flow into them. While some wastes are deadly, others are rich in nutrients that fertilize wetland plants, which in turn feed wetland animals.

Then, too, many wetlands are wholesome recreational areas where people can enjoy a variety of activities such as boating, fishing, bird-watching, and nature walks. And painters, writers, photographers, and other artists have been inspired by visiting these beautiful, and sometimes mysterious, places.

OUR DISAPPEARING WETLANDS

When Europeans first came to North America, there were over 200 million acres (81 million hectares) of wetlands in what is now the continental United States (this does not include Alaska and Hawaii). Today, less than 95 million acres (38 million ha) remain.

Another 200 million acres of wetlands exist in Alaska as *tundra,* or frozen wetland that has a permanent layer of ice beneath the surface. Tundra is a nesting place for a variety of ducks and geese, as well as many other waterbirds such as sandpipers, loons, and gulls.

Most of the wetlands in the continental United States are found in the upper Midwest, the Southeast and Gulf Coast, and along the Northeastern coastal states. About 95 percent of our wetlands are inland; the rest are coastal.

Throughout the nation, we are losing about half a

Above: The Alaskan tundra is a wetland area with a permanent layer of ice beneath the surface. The tundra has no trees, but lichens, mosses, and grasses provide some food and cover for wildlife.

Left: The tundra is home to many waterbirds, such as this Arctic tern.

A number of wetlands that have
been cleared for navigation
channels are now endangered.

million acres (202,000 ha) of wetlands every year. Many wetlands have been cleared, mainly for farmland. Others have been drained to make room for homes and industrial complexes. Wetlands have also been cleared to build channels for navigation, as well as *levees*—wide walls along riverbanks—and dams for flood control. Natural causes, like erosion and storms, also destroy wetlands.

Today, many wetlands in the United States are endangered. These include the prairie pothole region in the Midwest; the Lower Mississippi flood plain in Louisiana, Mississippi, and Arkansas; the Kissimmee River, Lake Okeechobee, and the Everglades system in south Florida; and the Western riparian areas in the Southwestern and Western states. Each time a wetland vanishes, we lose another natural resource with the wildlife that it supports.

WHAT LIVES IN THE WETLANDS?

LIFE IN THE SWAMPS

Bird life and plant life are especially rich in the tree-filled wetlands known as *swamps*. Some swamps are quite small, while others, such as the Everglades in Florida, the Okefenokee in Florida and Georgia, and the Atchafalaya in Louisiana, are extensive.

SWAMP PLANTS   Bald cypress trees, water tupelo, custard apple, and pop ash are some swampland trees. Bald cypress got its name because its delicate needles are shed yearly. This leaves the tree bare except for gray, stringy masses of Spanish moss that dangle from its branches. Spanish moss is one of many "air plants" that grow on the trunks and branches of swampland trees.

A variety of ferns and flowers are also swamp

Above: Cypress trees in the Atchafalaya swamp in Louisiana can grow up to 120 feet (35 m) tall.

Left: Spanish moss dangles from many of the swampland trees. It is called an air plant because it has no roots and gets its food and moisture from the air.

dwellers. Perhaps the strangest swampland fern is the resurrection fern. This plant looks dead until half an hour after a rainfall. Then it springs back to life, green and beautiful.

Among the flowers that decorate and give their fragrance to swamps are orchids, wild hibiscus, spider lilies, and wild gardenias. As in marshes, you will find low-lying shrubs here, especially around the edges of the swamp.

SWAMP ANIMALS

A remarkable variety of rare and exquisite birds nest in swamps, often in colonies high up in secluded trees. Here are wood storks, herons, roseate spoonbills, and other wading birds. California wrens, cardinals, and red-shouldered hawks are some more swampland residents, while wood thrushes and warblers are among the songbirds that migrate here for part of the year.

Amphibians such as salamanders and frogs live here, too. So do many reptiles. These include turtles, and snakes such as the sluggish but poisonous cottonmouth, named for the white lining inside its mouth. Another swamp dweller is the alligator, North America's largest reptile. Although dangerous, alligators are also the unsung heroes of the American Southeast swamps they inhabit. They create pits that fill with water, which fish, turtles, wading birds, and mammals

Left: Spider lilies are often found in swamps.

Below: The spoonbill, ibis, and snowy egret are wading birds that nest in the wetlands.

use in dry seasons. (A refuge for the alligator's close and endangered relative, the crocodile, was recently established on Key Largo in Florida.)

Raccoons, deer, foxes, and gray squirrels are among the mammals that inhabit swamps. The mysterious Florida panther, which lives in Florida's Everglades and Big Cypress Swamp, is nearly extinct because of the loss of its habitat.

Many of the same insects that live here, such as mosquitoes, dragonflies, and damselflies, also live in freshwater marshes. In both places, they are a valuable food source for larger animals.

As in every other natural habitat, each animal in the swamp is linked to every other animal in a food chain which often has many steps, from the tiniest food-producing plants to the largest meat-eating swamp dwellers. In wetlands like these, the food chain usually starts with simple plants called *algae*, as well as with *detritus*, a thick, high-protein vegetable stew of decaying plants and small animals. Detritus is easily digested by small creatures, which in turn are eaten by larger ones.

FRESHWATER MARSHES

In the United States, our inland marshes can be seen in such places as Delaware's Bombay Hook National

Left: Alligators, North America's largest reptiles, inhabit the Everglades and other southeastern swamps.

Below: The Florida panther is endangered because much of its natural swamp habitat has been destroyed.

Wildlife Refuge, North Dakota's Upper Souris National Wildlife Refuge, and Utah's Bear River Migratory Bird Refuge. A smaller marsh may be right in your own neighborhood.

FRESHWATER MARSH PLANTS

Sedges, grasses, cattails, and rushes are the most typical plants in freshwater marshes. Thick stands of these plants offer superior food, shelter, and breeding areas for many animals. Marshes also contain an array of wild flowers, including duckweed. The high nutritional value of this tiny flowering plant supplies much of the dietary needs of waterfowl and muskrats.

Many marsh plants have been used for centuries by North American Indians for both food and medicinal purposes. These plants include the cattails, whose roots, seeds, and stems are eaten, and pickleweed, which is served in a salad. (Deer, ducks, and muskrats also eat pickleweed.) North American Indians reduce fevers with a tea made from black willow, treat diarrhea with purple loosestrife, and take care of poison ivy with jewelweed, all freshwater marsh plants.

FRESHWATER MARSH ANIMALS

Although many animals live in freshwater marshes, the best known is probably the duck. Many species of these lovable birds are endangered today, as their wet-

Cattails are a common freshwater marsh plant.
Their thick growth provides cover for small birds
and other wetlands animals.

land habitats disappear. Other freshwater marsh birds include the great blue heron, the black tern, and the ducklike grebes, which dive into the water like winged torpedoes. That superb hunter, the marsh hawk, as well as red-winged blackbirds, and rails, coots, and gallinules are some more marsh residents.

Amphibians are primarily represented by a variety of frogs. Reptiles include snakes and turtles, like the snapping turtle, and the spiny soft-shell turtle. Numerous fish, such as perch, striped bass, and catfish, also make freshwater marshes their homes. Hard-shelled animals, including clams and crayfishes, live here, too. And the marsh wouldn't be complete without plenty of insects in season, from mosquitoes to midges, which serve as food for other animals.

If you are looking for mammals in a freshwater marsh, you may spot meadow jumping mice and marsh rabbits on the muddy ground or catch a glimpse of minks, otters, beavers, and muskrats swimming through the water. Other mammals living near or in marshlands include coyotes, javelinas, bobcats, raccoons, and foxes, as well as bears, the largest freshwater marsh animals.

While a freshwater marsh is just murky water and mosquitoes to some people, it is a wonderland to those who appreciate the complex wildlife community it supports.

Above: The great blue heron
lives in freshwater marshes.

Left: The otter is part
of the wildlife community in
a freshwater marsh.

SALTWATER MARSHES

Saltwater marshes fringe the North American coastline. They are found along the Atlantic, Gulf, Pacific, and Alaskan coasts. Within them live distinct wildlife species that can survive in areas of changing tides and high levels of *salinity*, or saltiness. Our country's saltwater marshes include Louisiana's Sabine National Wildlife Refuge, South Carolina's Cape Romain National Wildlife Refuge, and Virginia's Chincoteague National Wildlife Refuge, where wild horses add to its beauty.

SALTWATER MARSH PLANTS

The greatest source of food for all saltwater marsh animals is the marsh grasses. The most important of these is cordgrass. While most rooted plants can't live in salt water, cordgrasses thrive in it, and provide shelter and food for many animals.

People are often surprised to find that many saltwater marsh wild flowers are very colorful when in bloom. Sea lavender has lovely lavender-pink flowers in late summer. Seaside goldenrod adds yellow to the scenery from June to December. Sea milkwort, an early bloomer, has white, pink, or purple flowers, while swamp rose mallow displays white or pink flowers all summer long. These and other wildflowers each have a special place in the marsh, depending on how much salt they can tolerate.

Virginia's Chincoteague Wildlife Refuge is a large
saltwater marsh famous for its wild horses.
Here several drink from one of the freshwater
canals that crisscross the refuge.

Like the waters of freshwater marshes, waters in saltwater marshes are filled with detritus. This is eaten by many small creatures that are then eaten by larger animals, including millions of shorebirds.

SALTWATER MARSH ANIMALS

Many types of shorebirds and wading birds stalk the shallows of saltwater marshes. Clapper rails, herons, and egrets are all most active at low tide, when they poke their beaks into the mud for food. They often dine on small fish, insects, and snails, as well as oysters, crabs, and mussels, which filter detritus from the water around them.

Amphibians are generally missing from very salty areas, but reptiles in this bustling community may include the brown snake, the diamondback terrapin, and the loggerhead turtle. Rabbits, mice, rats, raccoons, and opossums are some of the mammals that frequent saltwater marshes.

ESTUARIES: VERY SPECIAL PLACES

As we travel to or from the seacoast, we reach a place where freshwater from rivers and streams mixes with seawater. This is the estuary, among Mother Earth's most vital fish habitats. Some fish spend their entire lives here. Others, born in the sea, swim here as adults to munch on small edibles such as shrimp and crabs. Still other fish, like the salmon, swim through estuaries on their way from the sea to the freshwater habitats where they will spawn, or lay their eggs.

Estuaries make safe nurseries for many ocean fish. Food is abundant here, and the mixed waters protect baby fish from their less adaptable ocean enemies. One-half to two-thirds of the valuable food fish netted along the Atlantic and Pacific coasts spend part of their lives in estuaries. Here, too, you may find the Florida manatee, a large and gentle endangered mammal now found only in Florida.

Like freshwater marshes, saltwater marshes are valuable to people as well as to wildlife. Their grasses act as barriers to help protect beaches from eroding and flooding. They also filter the water that runs through them. Despite these benefits, our saltwater marshes are disappearing at an alarming rate.

They have been prime targets for housing developments, since many people want to live by the sea. Engineered flood controls, along with pollution from industry, have also taken their toll. As saltwater marshes vanish, the balance of nature is upset.

The large, gentle Florida manatee is an
endangered mammal. Often called a sea cow,
it feeds on aquatic plants.

In Florida's far south, saltwater marshes become saltwater swamplands filled with mangrove trees. White mangroves and black mangroves are farther upland, where it is less salty, while red mangroves triumph in the saltiest conditions. Forests of red mangroves help save the coast from surging storm waves by absorbing floodwater and releasing it slowly.

At the same time, the mangroves' extensive tangle of overground roots shelters land and marine animals. These roots trap sediments efficiently enough to build up new land. Over the last forty years, they have added 1,500 acres (600 ha) to Florida's coastline.

When the mangrove leaves and twigs fall into the water and decompose, their nutrients begin forming detritus. The smaller fish and shellfish feed on the detritus, and are in turn eaten by bigger fish, such as mangrove snappers and tarpons, as well as by crabs and birds.

A COMEBACK FOR THE WETLANDS

Over the last few decades, people have become better informed about the value of our wetlands. Throughout the country, environmentalists are trying to get laws passed that will protect these wonderlands from being cleared and filled in. But the battle has barely begun.

Until recently, whatever protection the wetlands had came from part of the Clean Water Act of 1972, which prohibits filling any water area without a permit from the United States Army Corps of Engineers. This federal agency oversees all the waters of our country. In 1988, the administration urged that a "no net loss of wetlands" policy be adopted. Should this policy go into effect, it would require developers who fill in a wetlands area to restore or create an equal amount of wetlands elsewhere.

The "no net loss" principle is still not the perfect solution because it has many loopholes. And because their profits are affected, many corporate farmers, developers, and oil companies are spending millions of dollars to actively oppose saving the wetlands. Also, many wetlands are totally unique and cannot be replaced.

But the future is bright. Today, in some places, government agencies, developers, scientists, and environmentalists are starting to work together to protect and preserve our dying wetlands. And, as you will see from the cases that follow, their efforts are beginning to have an impact.

THE WHOOPING CRANE: A BITTERSWEET SUCCESS STORY

One of the most magnificent of all marshland dwellers is the whooping crane, or whooper. Once almost extinct, these endangered birds now face a new battle in their wetland homes.

Whoopers are fascinating creatures. Adults have beautiful white feathers trimmed in black at the wingtips, and a bright-red crown where their skin is exposed. They are the tallest birds in North America, standing up to 6 feet (1.8 m) tall. They are also among the highest-flying birds on earth. Whoopers can weigh as much as 25 pounds (11 kg), and can live for over 30 years. Their 110-decibel trumpetlike call, "kee-loo, ker-lee-oo," can be heard for up to 3 miles (5 km) away.

Like all other cranes, whoopers mate for life. Each new couple performs a courtship dance, gracefully bowing their heads, spreading their wings, and leaping into the air together. Later, when the eggs that the female whooper lays hatch, both parents will help to raise their fuzzy, cinnamon-colored chicks.

Some scientists estimate that when Europeans first came to America, about 1,400 whoopers lived here. Many nested across much of the northern plains in the summer and wintered along the Gulf Coast. But, by the late 1930s, there were no more than twenty-five birds making their annual 2,600-mile (4,200-km) migration between northwestern Canada and the Texas coast.

A major reason for the decline of whoopers was the loss of their marshland homes. As people drained these wetlands for human use, the birds were left without safe places for nesting and eating. Many whoopers also were lost to early 1900s hunters, who shot them for their fine feathers, which were used in making women's hats.

In 1937, the whoopers' wintering grounds in Texas was made into the Aransas National Wildlife Refuge, protected by the U.S. Fish and Wildlife Service. In the mid-1950s, when the whoopers' summer breeding ground was found in Canada, they gained legal protection from that country, too.

To help the whoopers even more, scientists set up a

A pair of whooping cranes performing their
unique courtship dance. Each pair of
whoopers requires a territory of about
400 acres to support them.

captive breeding program. Whooper females in the wild lay two eggs, but only one of every two chicks that hatch reaches adulthood. So scientists began shipping one egg from each whooper's nest to a research center in Maryland. There, some whooper eggs were given to nonendangered sandhill cranes, who became the whoopers' foster parents. Other eggs were incubated by machine, and the hatchlings were raised by humans. This helped the whooper population grow.

Now, with each whooper pair in Canada having only one chick to bring up in the wild, the young have a better chance of surviving. The birds are also helped by a crane-spotting network that tracks them as they migrate to and from Canada.

Today, we have two captive whooper flocks, with a total of fifty-four birds. These are at the Patuxent Research Center in Maryland and the International Crane Foundation in Wisconsin. But the only wild breeding flock of whoopers winters in the wetlands of Aransas. Here the whooper population has been rising steadily, with a record high of 146 birds in 1990. However, Aransas itself is now endangered.

Each year, over 3,000 barges use the waterway running through the wetlands. Many barges carry tanks of dangerous chemicals. A chemical spill or a crash between two barges could quickly destroy almost every wild whooping crane. A major spill from the oil barges is another threat. Even if an oil spill doesn't kill the birds, it might destroy their food supply, forcing them to leave the safety of the refuge.

Aransas has other problems. Deepening the harbor created artificial islands that cover marshes the cranes once used. And the wake from water traffic is causing as many as 3 acres (1.2 ha) of marsh to vanish each year. Another big concern is water pollution.

The U.S. Fish and Wildlife Service and the state of Texas are presently trying to create more wintering areas around Aransas for its growing whooper flock. And the Canadian and United States governments are planning to set up a nonmigratory wild flock in the United States. But the whoopers' future is still unsure. And as is true of the whooping crane, no wetland inhabitant will be safe until the wetlands are safe.

SAVING THE DWINDLING DUCK FACTORY

A world without ducklings each spring? This may be difficult to imagine, but in fact, North America's duck population has greatly plummeted due to the loss of wetlands in our country's prairie pothole region. This area, including parts of Montana, North and South Dakota, and Minnesota, is known as North America's duck factory. Over 50 percent of the continent's ducks nest here.

Water traffic can erode and pollute wetlands,
endangering them and the wildlife
that depends on them.

So many of these potholes have been converted into farmland that many ducks face great danger. Food is scarce in ditched marshes. Furthermore, when the marshes are too dry, smoldering fires start in them, killing both duck eggs and ducklings. Because of these dangers, species like the redhead and canvasback ducks are seriously endangered.

In 1986, the United States and Canada adopted the North American Waterfowl Management Plan. The main goal of this plan is to restore wetland conditions and duck numbers to what they were in the early 1970s. The hope is that it is not too late to save our ducks and other prairie pothole inhabitants.

SAVING LOUISIANA'S WETLANDS

Louisiana, which has 40 percent of the nation's coastal wetlands, is facing a major crisis. When left alone, wetlands function as natural flood controls. However, in Louisiana, flood controls, as well as navigation channels, have been built all along the Mississippi River, which feeds the state's marshes. Due to such engineering feats, as much as 50 square miles (130 sq km) of Louisiana's coastal marshes sink into the Gulf of Mexico each year. Further upland, one of the world's largest bottomland forests is rapidly shrinking.

The disappearing wetlands of Montana
and neighboring states are the main nesting
areas of North America's ducks.

These losses greatly jeopardize wildlife in Louisiana. As the bottomwood forests recede, the black bears that live in them are heading for the endangered species list. Nearer the sea, natural nurseries for 80 percent of the fish and shellfish that swim from the Atlantic Ocean into the Gulf of Mexico are threatened.

The huge flocks of birds that live or stop here during their migrations are also in jeopardy. And wetland destruction affects many people, including those who live off the fish, shellfish, wild rice, and other foods that are found in wetlands along the delta area at the mouth of the Mississippi River.

Today, numerous citizens' groups in the Mississippi River area are meeting with developers and officials at every level of government. They are exploring ways to heal the wounds already made in the land, and to prevent new bruises from appearing.

SAVING THE EVERGLADES

Florida's 2,796-square-mile (7,242-sq-km) Everglades area is known as both a swamp and a "river of grass." This slow-moving river, filled with saw grass and other vegetation, shelters and feeds some of earth's rarest and most beautiful wildlife. On a visit here, you may catch a glimpse of gorgeous wading birds, as well as the endangered crocodile, Florida panther, bald eagle, and

Everglades kite. But today there is no longer the abundance of plants and animals that once shared this unique habitat.

In the early 1900s, people began draining large areas of the Everglades to build a network of canals, dams, and levees all the way from the Kissimmee River, the Everglades' origin of water, to the ocean. People wanted to farm on the wetlands' rich soil, and pave other parts of it for urban developments. In the 1940s the region was "improved" on a much grander scale. Such tampering has drastically altered the Glades' natural water flow.

Now, during droughts, water goes to urban areas first, while the Glades stay thirsty. And the wetlands' rich muck soil, once called "black gold," has turned out to be "fool's gold." When the muck dries, it burns easily, and upon exposure to air it blows away. These problems are dooming farms in the area.

Also, as a result of engineering, seawater is creeping into home wells. Expensive water desalting devices must be used to make the water usable for humans. Some experts expect the lack of fresh drinking water to eventually become a crisis in southern Florida. Pollution, primarily from big dairy and sugarcane farms, is another huge concern for the Glades.

Today, efforts are growing to save the Glades. There are plans to expand the Everglades National Park so that more land will come under national park status.

This water control gate is part
of a system regulating the flow
of water into the Everglades.

Another project under way will open some upstream canals and bring a more natural water flow to parts of the Glades.

Like other vanished wetlands, the Glades can never be the same. Although there is nothing else like it on earth, 50 percent of the Glades has already vanished, along with over 90 percent of the area's wading birds. But, hopefully, as citizens' groups and government agencies become more actively involved in saving the Glades, the health of this wilderness paradise will improve.

SAVING SAN FRANCISCO BAY

In California, many people are trying to protect San Francisco Bay, the state's largest estuary. For the last thirty years, it has been regulated by the San Francisco Bay Conservation and Development Commission. When the commission began, 90 percent of the bay's tidal marshes had already been lost. Today, the commission, and many environmentalist groups, are working to influence public opinion so that the estuary is not further ruined. Despite these efforts, the Bay remains at risk.

Fresh water is currently being diverted to supply the tremendous demand from southern California. This upsets the estuary system, which needs just the right

The Florida Everglades area resembles
a slow-moving river of grass.

The Arcata Marsh and Wildlife Sanctuary in California
was developed as a wetlands filter system that
helps to purify wastewater. This successful project is
now home to two hundred species of birds.

balance of fresh water and salt water. Pollution and dredging projects from industrial developments also threaten it, and require citizens' groups to stay on constant guard against new threats.

TRANSFORMING A "WASTELAND"

When the townspeople of Arcata, California, needed a sewage treatment plant to purify the wastewater flowing into their bay, they turned to nature. They created a wetlands filter system by converting abandoned land into 96 acres (39 ha) of wetlands.

The marshes began filtering wastewater in 1986. Today, water entering the bay is cleaner than that discharged from a regular treatment plant. This natural process is also much less expensive. And, as an added bonus, the new Arcata Marsh and Wildlife Sanctuary is home to two hundred species of birds, and a treat for nature lovers. The Arcata project has been so successful that it is being studied as a model for other communities.

As we learn more about the wetlands, we will devise even more creative ways to work with them rather than against them. And someday, perhaps you will help provide fresh ideas that will enable us to make wiser use of our living planet's precious wetlands.

WELCOME TO
THE MARSHES

The best way to discover the treasures of the marshes is to visit them. However, these soggy places may have hidden dangers, so be sure to explore them with an adult who is familiar with the area. And read the following list. It will help make your explorations safer and more satisfying.

☐ Wear high, waterproof boots or old sneakers, as well as old pants. Apply insect repellent. Bring along one or more sealable containers for collecting specimens. You may also want to carry a magnifying glass, binoculars, a spoon, and an eyedropper.

☐ If you are a bird watcher, visit a freshwater marsh in early morning or around sunset, and a saltwater marsh when the tide is low. Birds are most active at these times.

☐ Respect nature at all times, and shhhh! Walk very quietly, and watch for hidden birds' nests before stepping into grassy areas.

☐ If you step down into a hole, lift your feet up slowly, so you don't lose your boots or shoes.

☐ Stay off any floating plant mats. Since these are not solid, you might sink into the water. Instead, walk on the side of them.

☐ Look below the water at the busy wildlife communities there. You may want to collect some creatures to bring home for further study. Examine other creatures on the spot, then carefully put them back where you found them.

☐ You can collect bigger, more-familiar plants, like cattails and bulrushes. But leave the smaller plants alone, since many of them are endangered.

☐ Do *not* taste any plants. Some wetland plants are poisonous. These include marsh marigold, water hemlock, swamp hellebore, and arrow arum.

☐ Learn to recognize wetland plants that are dangerous to touch. You can get oozing, itchy blisters from poison ivy, with its three leaves and white berries. Touching the stem and leaves of showy lady's slipper, a lovely-looking wildflower with white and rose flowers, can give you a blistering rash. So can the marsh butter-cup. And the root of the blue flag, a member of the iris family, can irritate your skin.

☐ When you get home, wash thoroughly. Check your body for ticks. If you think that you have come in contact with poison ivy, scrub the affected skin with soap and water. Then swab alcohol over the area and apply a paste of baking soda and water.

APPENDIX

Cooperative Whooping Crane Tracking Project, Project Leader, U.S. Fish and Wildlife Service, 2604 St. Patrick, Suite 7, Grand Island, NE 68803. (Write to learn how to become involved as an observer.)

Ducks Unlimited, #1 Waterfowl Way, Long Groves, IL 60047

National Audubon Society, 950 Third Avenue, New York, NY 10022

National Audubon Society Wetlands Campaign, Sharon, CT 06069

National Wetlands Conservation Project, c/o Nature Conservancy, 1800 North Kent Street, Suite 800, Arlington, VA 22209

National Wildlife Federation, 1400 Sixteenth Street NW, Washington, DC 20036–2266

Sierra Club, 330 Pennsylvania Avenue SE, Washington, DC 20003

U.S. Fish and Wildlife Service Publication Unit, 1717 H Street NW, Room 148, Washington DC 20006

Whooping Crane Conservation Association, Sierra Vista, AZ 85635. (Established in 1961. Annual dues are $5. Members receive newsletter four times a year.)

Check your Yellow Pages for local chapters of many of these national organizations. Also check the local office of the U.S. Fish and Wildlife Service.

PLACES TO SEE WETLANDS IN THE UNITED STATES

Some Places to See Saltwater Marshes:
California—Elkhorn Slough Estuary Sanctuary
Florida—Gulf Islands National Seashore
Louisiana—Sabine National Wildlife Refuge
Maryland—Assateague Island National Seashore
Massachusetts—Parker River National Wildlife Refuge
New Jersey—Brigantine National Wildlife Refuge
North Carolina—Cape Hatteras National Seashore
Oregon—South Slough Estuarine Sanctuary
South Carolina—Cape Romain National Wildlife Refuge
Texas—Aransas National Wildlife Refuge
Virginia—Chincoteague National Wildlife Refuge

Some Places to See Freshwater Marshes:
California—Lower Klamath and Tule Lake National Wildlife refuges
Delaware—Bombay Hook National Wildlife Refuge
Idaho—Camas National Wildlife Refuge
Maine—Moosehorn National Wildlife Refuge
Massachusetts—Great Meadows National Wildlife Refuge
Minnesota—Agassiz National Wildlife Refuge
Montana—Red Rock Lakes National Wildlife Refuge
Nevada—Ruby Lake National Wildlife Refuge
New York—Montezuma National Wildlife Refuge
North Dakota—Upper Souris National Wildlife Refuge

Oregon—Malheur National Wildlife Refuge
Utah—Bear River Migratory Bird Refuge

Some Places to See Cypress Swamps:
Florida—Big Cypress Swamp; Corkscrew Swamp Sanctuary; Wakulla Springs
Georgia—Okefenokee National Wildlife Refuge
North Carolina—Croatan National Forest; Great Dismal Swamp
South Carolina—Francis Marion National Forest
Tennessee—Reelfoot State Park
Virginia—Great Dismal Swamp

GLOSSARY

ALGAE.   A variety of primitive, chiefly water, plants that are often at the bottom of the food chain in wetlands.

BOG.   Often a forerunner of swamps. Bogs are poorly drained spongy areas that are rich in mosses and partially decayed plant life called peat.

BOTTOMLANDS.   The forested lowlands along streams and rivers.

CANAL.   An artificial waterway used for irrigation, travel, and shipping.

CHANNEL.   A deep navigable passageway through water.

DAM.   A barrier built across a body of water to control its flow or raise the level of the water.

DETRITUS.   Decayed matter that, like algae, is an important primary producer in the wetlands' food chain.

DREDGING.   The process of clearing out the bottom of a body of water so that ships can pass through.

ECOLOGY.   The study of environments and the individual life-forms that are found there.

ECOSYSTEMS. The environments themselves, along with the life-forms that dwell in them.

ENVIRONMENTALIST. Someone concerned about preserving earth's natural areas and the wildlife that inhabit them.

ESTUARIES. Places where salt water from the sea mixes with fresh water from rivers.

FLOOD PLAIN. A plain bordering a river that is subject to flooding.

FOOD CHAIN. The chain of living things in a community in which each link in the chain feeds on a link below it and is fed upon by the one above it.

HABITAT. The particular kind of ecosystem to which a species has adapted.

LEVEE. An embankment, often made from sandbags, to prevent a river from overflowing.

MARSH. A treeless wetland generally characterized by cattails and sedges.

PRAIRIE POTHOLE. Shallow, marshlike pond located mainly in the Midwest.

RIPARIAN. Wetlands along any inland body of water.

SALINITY. Degree of salt in water.

SATURATED. Soaked with moisture.

SEDGES. Grasslike plants that have solid stems instead of hollow ones such as grasses.

SEDIMENT. Pieces of matter suspended in water.

SPHAGNUM. A type of moss usually found in a bog.

SWAMP. Wetland characterized by trees.

TUNDRA. Frozen wetland found in northern climates.

FOR FURTHER READING

Cortesi, Wendy. *Explore a Spooky Swamp*. Washington, D.C.: National Geographic Society, 1978.

Kennedy, Carolyn L. *Exploring Wildlife Communities with Children*. New York: Girl Scouts of the U.S.A., 1981.

Lampton, Christopher. *Endangered Species*. New York: Franklin Watts, 1988.

Parker, Steve. *Pond & River*. New York: Alfred A. Knopf, 1988.

Patent, Dorothy Hinshaw. *The Whooping Crane, A Comeback Story*. New York: Clarion Books, 1988.

Pringle, Laurence. *Estuaries: Where Rivers Meet the Sea*. New York: Macmillan, 1973.

Roop, Peter and Connie. *Seasons of the Cranes*. New York: Walker, 1989.

Williams, Terry Tempest. *Between Cattails*. New York: Scribner, 1985.

Recommended Advanced Reading
Lyons, Janet, and Sandra Jordan. *Walking the Wetlands*. New York: Wiley, 1989.

INDEX